MORE POWER TOOLS for Teaching

BETH LEFGREN

JENNIFER JACKSON

Illustrated by Brent Palmer

BOOKCRAFT
Salt Lake City, Utah

Library of Congress Catalog Card Number: 90-85260

ISBN 0-88494-780-7

3rd Printing, 1994

Printed in the United States of America

Contents

Preface

You've probably already noticed that object lessons are "in"! Everywhere you look you find people using them to get a point across. Object lessons are being used to help people visualize ideas in everything from TV drug commercials to general conference.

As we were putting this book together we noticed how contemporary many of the subjects were. It was great to see object lessons about program changes, stress, fellowshipping, correlation, teaching—all subjects of concern in today's world. It was also nice to see how many new object lessons are available in the "always necessary" subjects—faith, love, goals, service, repentance, and reverence.

One of the nice things about an object lesson is that no two people will use it in exactly the same way. So we have tried to keep each one basic enough for personal creativity and yet versatile enough to fit many occasions.

All of us are teachers at some time. So don't hesitate to use object lessons in all your teaching experiences—home, classroom, or community. We've found that the more you use them the better you get as a teacher. We hope that you will find these object lessons useful and that you will find success in the most important job anyone could have—teaching.

Activation

Objective: To show how the right preparation is important in friendshipping.

Materials Needed: Two pots, dirt, two carrots (greens attached), and a hand spade.

Preparation: "Plant" a carrot in each pot. Make sure that the dirt in each pot is *firmly* packed around the carrot.

Procedure: Take out the two potted carrots and show them to the class. Liken each carrot to an inactive or nonmember person. Have a class member come up and yank on the greens of one carrot (this will leave the carrot in the potted dirt). Explain that when we try to pull, push, or force someone into activity, we are usually unsuccessful.

Now focus on the other potted carrot. Begin to work the soil with the hand spade. Tell the class that when we loosen the soil around the carrot it will be easier to lift the carrot gently out. Remind the class that care must be taken so the carrot will not be bruised or damaged during the process.

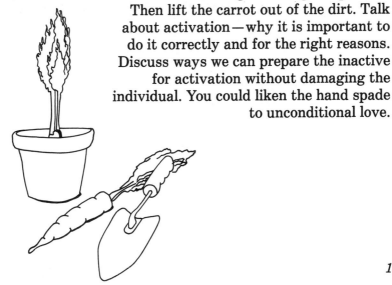

Then lift the carrot out of the dirt. Talk about activation—why it is important to do it correctly and for the right reasons. Discuss ways we can prepare the inactive for activation without damaging the individual. You could liken the hand spade to unconditional love.

Adversity

Objective: To illustrate that a strong testimony can help us to deal with adversity.

Materials Needed: Two paper sacks (carefully unseal the bottom seam of one) and three or four lemons.

Procedure: Hold up the sack with the unsealed bottom and explain that it represents a person who doesn't have a strong testimony. Show a lemon and tell them it represents the adversity that everyone experiences in life. Drop the lemons one by one into the bag, pointing out that when our testimonies are not strong we are not able to deal effectively with the adversity.

Contrast this by holding up the other bag and likening it to a person with a steadfast testimony. Drop the lemons into the bag one by one, then fold the opening of the bag and shake it. Point out that those with strong testimonies can cope with a great deal of adversity.

All of us are given lemons from time to time in our lives. Whether or not we can cope with the stress they place on us may depend on our testimonies.

Apostasy

Objective: To illustrate how gospel ordinances can be changed.

Materials Needed: One glass of canal water and one glass of spring water.

Procedure: Show the two glasses of water. Ask what the differences are. Explain that one glass (hold up the clear water) comes from the source and is pure and crystal clear. Hold up the glass of canal water and explain that at one time this water was clean but as it traveled many miles from the source it became dirty and gathered impurities. If you wish, talk about what kinds of pollutions could have been picked up by the water.

Liken the water to ordinances in the gospel of Jesus Christ. When the ordinances come from the source (Jesus Christ) they are pure and simple, but the further from the source the more impure and complex the ordinances become. Take a moment and discuss what might change the clarity of ordinances and make them impure.

Attitude

Objective: To show that things are accomplished best when we are in the right frame of mind.

Materials Needed: A paintbrush, water-base red paint, water-base black paint, a can of water, and paper.

Procedure: Load your brush with red paint and begin to paint a picture. Explain that the picture you are painting is like a goal and by using the red paint you will try to effectively achieve that goal. Talk about how the black paint is like negatives that arise while you are working toward a goal. If you desire, discuss what kind of negatives can affect a goal. As you discuss this dip the brush into the black paint. Lightly rinse the black brush, but not completely.

Tell the class that when a negative comes along it can leave residue. Now dip the brush back into the red paint and paint on the paper (there should be enough residual black to make the color murky).

Explain to the class that just as the brush must be thoroughly rinsed, we must get rid of *all* negatives before we can effectively and completely achieve our goals.

Attitude

Objective: To show that how we view things reflects our attitude.

Materials Needed: One half-filled glass of water.

Procedure: Place the glass of water on a table where it can be seen by everyone. Ask each person in the class to describe what he or she sees. Be sure that each member has a chance to respond. Some people will perceive the glass as half full while others will view it as half empty.

Explain that how we view things can reflect our attitudes. If we try to view things positively, we will see the glass as half full of water. If we let the negative prevail, we will see the glass as half empty. Remind the class that a negative outlook on life can be replaced with a positive frame of mind. Discuss why a positive point of view can be important.

Remember to keep your lesson positive!

Balanced Living

Objective: To show how balance is important in our lives.

Materials Needed: A three-legged stool.

Procedure: Show the stool to the class and ask what would happen if one of the legs was shorter or longer than the other two.

Explain that our lives are like the stool and need to be balanced equally in three areas; self-improvement, family relations, and church activity. When we become stronger or weaker in one of these areas our lives can become unbalanced and we might be easily tipped over. Discuss what must be done to keep our lives in balance.

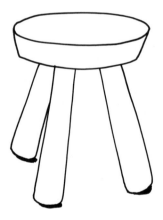

Balanced Living

Objective: To help us realize the value of balancing the activities in our lives.

Materials Needed: A cardboard box, several heavy books, a glass pitcher, and several towels.

Procedure: Show the class the items you have brought. Tell them that if you were to move you would need to pack your household items. Discuss with the class how common sense should be used in packing (the box might be too heavy or something could be broken). Ask what might happen if common sense is not used. Answers may include hurting yourself by trying to carry too heavy a load, requiring someone else's time to help you with the job, the bottom of the box breaking, a fragile item breaking. During the discussion, demonstrate and explain correct and incorrect packing.

Explain that the box is like our lives. At times we try to load too much into it. This can result in our becoming physically ill from overdoing it or in being so pressed for time that we have to call someone else to come and help with the workload. Other times we simply can't cope with the stress it has placed on us, and we suffer emotionally. There may even be times in our lives when, due to delicate circumstances, we can only carry one thing at a time. Discuss how we need to prayerfully fill our lives with those things which should be our priorities. By using wisdom and being in tune with the Spirit we can make our lives full, but the burden will not be so heavy that we cannot bear it.

Scripture Reference: Ecclesiastes 3:1–13; Mosiah 4:27.

Chastity

Objective: To illustrate why moral purity is important.

Materials Needed: A beat-up, dirty, rusty hanger; a new, unused hanger; and a beautiful, delicate article of clothing.

Procedure: Display the hangers and the clothing. Ask on which hanger you should hang the clothing. Discuss why.

Explain that when we allow our bodies or minds to be used in an unrighteous or worldly way our spirituality becomes dirty and rusty. Just as we would not want to hang our best and most delicate clothing on this hanger (hold up the dirty hanger), the Lord does not wish to cloak us with some very sacred, beautiful experiences (temple, priesthood) until our lives are in order and we are ready to receive them.

Additional Idea: This lesson leads into repentance very well by your showing the dirty hanger and discussing what could be done to make this hanger ready to be used again.

Choices

Objective: To show that we must make our own choices for good.

Materials Needed: Several nickels.

Procedure: Hold one of the nickels up and describe the two sides of the nickel. On a table, balance each coin on its edge. Ask one of the students to come up and carefully place each coin face up. Discuss how the student made deliberate choices to place the coins in a certain position.

Reposition the coins on their edges. Explain that, like the coins, we have two sides—positive and negative. We can usually make the choice that decides which side we will show the world. Sometimes, however, we allow outside influences (stress, fear, etc.) to make that decision for us (hit the table with your fist)—then things don't turn out quite the way we planned. Discuss ways that negative influences can be lessened or brought under control.

Choices

Objective: To encourage us to seek those things which are good for us.

Materials Needed: An apple and a cookie.

Procedure: Invite a group member to help you. Select someone whose strength is the same or less than yours. Have him raise his arm straight out to the side, shoulder level. Place the apple in his hand and instruct him to try to keep the arm in place as you apply pressure to push the arm down. Use two fingers and apply firm pressure to the arm. He will be able to keep it in place. Next replace the apple with the cookie and repeat the procedure exactly. The person's arm will have very little strength or resistance, and you will be able to push it down.

Use this to illustrate that choosing those things which are good for us will strengthen us. However, if we participate in or use things which are not good for us, we become weak and have less resistance to Satan.

Scripture Reference: Articles of Faith 1:13.

Communication

Objective: To demonstrate the effects of positive interaction with others.

Materials Needed: A piece of silver, a soft cloth, silver polish, and a powdered cleanser.

Procedure: Tell the class that you need to clean the silver and make it shiny and bright. Take the silver and the cloth and ask if you should use the powdered cleanser or the silver polish. Discuss what would result from using the cleanser (the silver would be discolored, marred, scratched; ruined, etc.). Compare the results of using the silver polish (wipe away smudges, keep the color bright, shine and value increased, etc.).

Explain that communication with others is like the silver and must be handled carefully. Gossiping, criticism, yelling and belittling are as harsh to a person as the powdered cleanser would have been to the silver. They can destroy another's self-esteem and confidence. This could result in temporarily or even permanently hampering a person's earthly progression.

Positive communication skills such as honest praise, recognition, soft voices, and uplifting vocabulary can be just as effective as the polish to the silver. Our methods of communication may be felt for many years after the original contact and can build another's self-worth or enhance their ability to achieve in life. We must carefully choose our words and actions.

Correlation

Objective: To show that correlation can help maintain a smooth and orderly Church program.

Materials Needed: A recording of a beautifully orchestrated piece of music.

Procedure: Play the music for several minutes. Ask the class how many people were necessary in putting together that piece of music. Be sure to include the orchestra members, conductor, and composer. Ask what would happen to the piece of music if there had been no composer, no director, no orchestra. Indicate how each member of the orchestra played an important part in the music.

Liken the piece of music to a ward in the Church.* Heavenly Father composed or organized the program. The bishop directs the organization and keeps it working in harmony. Each individual member of the ward needs to know and carry out his own responsibility. Express how important the individual members are in the function of the ward.

*Any organization can be used here. Substitute the correct officer as you give the lesson.

Dedication

Objective: To encourage us to increase our level of involvement in and dedication to worthwhile activities.

Materials Needed: A cake mix and a cake already prepared.

Procedure: Set out the cake mix and the cake for the class to see. Suggest that when they see the cake mix they might think about how good it would taste, but they would also think about the work involved in preparing it. Then have them look at the cake already prepared. Make sure it looks tempting. Suggest that now that they can see it and smell it, it becomes much more desirable and appealing. Slice a piece of it and give it to a class member and ask them to take a bite. Discuss how it's much more pleasurable to actually eat the cake than it is to simply look at the cake mix and think about it.

Liken this to any worthwhile activity. If we sit back and think about it, we are unable to enjoy the blessings it may hold for us. As we truly dedicate ourselves to the project, our level of enjoyment and satisfaction skyrockets.

Discernment

Objective: To show how easy it is to be deceived.

Materials Needed: A paper with an arrow drawn on it, and a mirror.

Procedure: Suggest that if we were to get lost, the most important thing we would need would be directions to point the way home. Hold up the arrow so that it points to either the right or the left. Explain that Heavenly Father gives us directions which we can trust will lead us back home. Satan desires to stop us from returning home. He will do anything he can to trick us and give us wrong directions.

Hold the mirror next to the arrow, angle them slightly towards each other so that the arrow is reflected in the mirror. The reflected image will point the opposite way the arrow points. Use this to illustrate how real Satan's deceptions can be, nevertheless they will not lead us home.

Emotions

Objective: To show that emotional hurt damages our ability to reflect the light of the gospel.

Materials Needed: A small hand mirror and an abrasive object.

Procedure: Show the class the mirror and ask how it might be used. (Be sure to include the fact that it reflects light or an image.) Now take the abrasive object and scratch the glass (reflective) side of the mirror. Show the class that, even though the mirror was scratched, its ability to reflect light and images has not been spoiled. Now turn the mirror over (painted side) and again scratch the mirror. Tell the class that the mirror has now been marred to the point of being unusable.

Explain that people are like the mirror. They can receive a physical (outward) injury and still function socially and spiritually, but when they sustain an emotional injury it can cause extensive damage, even the inability to reflect the light of Jesus Christ.

Additional Idea: You might want to discuss with the class what must be done to repair this damage (sanding and repainting). Liken this to unconditional love and fellowshipping.

Example

Objective: To illustrate how a positive example can help others.

Materials Needed: Two silver dollars, one tarnished and one shiny.

Procedure: Ask the class what they think will happen if the two coins are rubbed together. Invite comments.

Begin to rub the two coins together. As you are doing this, talk about how a positive, gospel-oriented person can set the example and eventually "rub-off" on associates and friends. Show the completed coins to the class (both coins will now shine) and invite a discussion of the topic.

Example

Objective: To encourage us to set a good example for others.

Materials Needed: A magnifying glass.

Procedure: Discuss with your class how the magnifying glass works. If your class is small enough, actually use the magnifying glass to view the tiny details of any object.

Explain that many times we as Church members are under a "magnifying glass" and our actions are under close inspection by nonmembers. Discuss the importance of setting a good example at all times.

Faith

Objective: To demonstrate the concept that faith is things though unseen believed in.

Materials Needed: A room with a door.

Procedure: Step out of the room and close the door. Leave the class members in the room. Now tell the class where you are. Ask if any of them can see you or if they can prove where you are. Step back into the room.

Liken each of these things to Heavenly Father. Heavenly Father tells us where he is through scripture and prophets. We can talk to him and he can talk to us through prayer and the promptings of the Holy Ghost. We cannot see him but we know that he's there.

Additional Idea: Discuss other things that cannot be seen but that we know are there (wind, fragrances, electricity, etc.).

Fellowshipping

Objective: To illustrate the value of fellowshipping nonmembers and less-active members.

Materials Needed: A balloon.

Procedure: Ask your group if they have ever tried to blow up a stiff balloon. It's difficult at best and sometimes impossible. By stretching and working with the balloon, we can make the process of blowing it up much easier.

We can liken this to fellowshipping nonmembers and less-active members. Trying to convert them or change them can be a difficult, nearly impossible task. By friend-shipping them, serving them, and setting a good example we can prepare them to receive the gospel in their lives.

Following Christ

Objective: To illustrate that we should follow the Savior.

Materials Needed: A vase of sunflowers or a picture of one.

Procedure: Show the sunflowers. Tell everyone that the sunflower waits patiently through the night until the sun appears for the day. Then the sunflower follows the course of the sun throughout the day and at nightfall it returns to its original position and waits for the sunrise.

Explain that we should be like the sunflower in our loyalty to and undeviating faith in the gospel of Jesus Christ. As we go through our life we should always keep our spiritual face focused on Jesus Christ as our Savior and Redeemer.

Following Christ

Objective: To encourage us to live Christ centered lives.

Materials Needed: A picture of our solar system.

Procedure: Display the picture of the solar system and explain that the sun is the center of our solar system with all the planets revolving around it. Discuss how rotation and revolution ensures our planet's constant light and heat.

Explain that the Savior offers us the spiritual light (truth) and warmth (love) that we need to guide us. Point out that to enjoy the full benefit of this we must keep him as the center of our lives. We can demonstrate his importance by revolving our lives around him. Discuss how this can be done (regular prayers, scripture study, meeting attendance, and daily actions).

Scripture Reference: John 8:12.

Following Christ

Objective: To show how we are protected from the ways of the world by following Christ.

Materials Needed: A carrot and a tomato.

Procedure: Display the carrot and tomato. Ask what would happen in a garden if a hard frost were to occur? (The tomato plant would die. The carrot, with its roots deep in the warm soil, would stay protected.)

Discuss how the evil ways of the world can destroy us spiritually. If we are living the gospel principles on the surface only, we are in danger. The only sure way of protecting ourselves is by closely following the teachings of Christ. This helps our spiritual roots to grow deep into the warm, loving protection which our Father in Heaven offers us.

Friendship

Objective: To show that our associations with other people can "rub off."

Materials Needed: Chalk dust.

Procedure: After "chalking" your hands, show them to the class. Ask the class what would happen if you shook hands with them or patted them on the back. Discuss.

Explain that friendship is much like the chalk dust. As we associate with friends, their good or bad qualities can rub off on us. Discuss how having a good friend can really support a person. Discuss what makes a friend.

Additional Idea: Discuss how to be a good friend and why it is important.

Goals

Objective: To illustrate how setting and working on goals is a step-by-step process.

Materials Needed: A large jigsaw puzzle.

Procedure: Ask if it would be possible for a member of the group to complete the puzzle in five minutes. Of course not; it would require sorting, studying, and carefully piecing it together. It may take a long time, but once you're done you'll have a beautiful picture and you will have enjoyed the process.

Point out that the same is true for setting and working on goals. It takes time to ponder and work on the goal. However, you will find yourself successfully completing your goal, and you will have a lot of enjoyment along the way.

Godhood

Objective: To help explain the ultimate goal of man in a simpler form.

Materials Needed: Pictures of a butterfly in its different stages (caterpillar, cocoon, butterfly).

Procedure: Show the pictures to the class. Discuss the various stages that a butterfly goes through. Tell the class that we do not understand how these changes take place but that we do know the end result.

Explain that we are like the caterpillar and that we have the potential of becoming like Heavenly Father. We may not understand how it takes place, but we do know the end result.

Additional Idea: Discuss what could keep a caterpillar from becoming a butterfly and compare that with what can keep us from becoming like Heavenly Father.

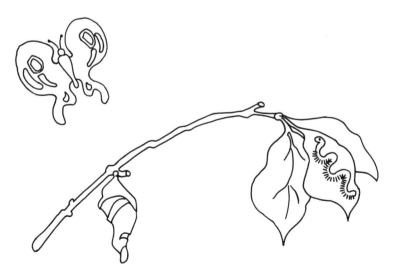

Gospel Living

Objective: To encourage us to always live the principles of the gospel.

Materials Needed: A coat.

Procedure: Explain that coats are designed to keep us warm and to protect us from the cold. Yet they can only offer us this service if we wear them. Sometimes we don't want to take the time to put one on; other times we don't want to be encumbered with one; and still other times we are embarrassed to wear one because it isn't quite fashionable. So we deny ourselves the comfort our coats could give us and instead we suffer with the cold.

Point out that living the principles of the gospel is similar to wearing a coat. The gospel can offer us protection and comfort from a cold world. Yet at times we won't make the effort to live the principles. Sometimes we feel that those principles are too restrictive or burdensome. And many times living by these standards isn't fashionable. So instead we suffer with the cold discomforts of a worldly life.

Gospel Living

Objective: To illustrate that the gospel must be more than an outward show.

Materials Needed: Several kinds of fruits and vegetables.

Preparation: Arrange the fruits and vegetables into a corsage or boutonniere.

Procedure: Walk into the classroom wearing the corsage or boutonniere. As a class member notices your unique decoration, take time to discuss its uses.

Tell the class that you have read that fruits and vegetables are an excellent source of vitamins and minerals and that you have decided to use them more often and improve your health. Allow the class to comment upon this. They will probably point out the inaccuracies of this statement. Ask them what must happen to the fruits and vegetables before you can achieve better health. (They must be eaten and become part of your body).

Explain that the gospel is like the fruits and vegetables. Wearing it on the outside (or partaking of it one day a week) will not help us to become spiritually healthy. Instead, we must consistently try to absorb the gospel until it becomes a part of us.

Gospel Living

Objective: To illustrate the importance of living the principles of the gospel every day.

Materials Needed: Bread, tuna, and jam.

Preparation: Make a sandwich using the jam and tuna as a filling.

Procedure: Show your class the sandwich and ask who would like to taste it. Generally speaking, the group will find the combination of jam and tuna undesirable. If the jam were removed, the sandwich would be completely edible.

Explain that our lives may be a similar offering to the Lord. We can attend church on Sunday, but if we live by worldly standards the rest of the week, it is as distasteful to the Lord as the tuna and jam sandwich was to the group. Discuss how we can be devoted disciples by living the gospel principles that we are learning.

Scripture Reference: Revelation 3:15–16.

Gospel Living

Objective: To show that gospel living must happen every day.

Materials Needed: Hair-care equipment (brush, dryer, curling iron, comb, etc.).

Procedure: Arrange the hair-care equipment on the table. Tell the class how much time you spent on your hair yesterday. Go into detail about how careful you were and how nice it looked and felt after you were through. Continue to tell the class that when you got up this morning you had to start all over. Briefly discuss this concept.

Explain that living the gospel is like doing your hair. No matter how much time the gospel took or how good it felt or even how in tune you were—it must be done all over again each day. True gospel living is a day-to-day activity.

Gospel Principles

Objective: To illustrate how gospel principles can protect us from the "fiery darts of the adversary."

Materials Needed: A can of insect repellent.

Procedure: Ask the class if they have ever camped out in a mosquito-infested area. As you discuss this experience, bring the class around to the feeling of being surrounded by many mosquitoes, each anxious to bite you. Show the can of repellent to the class and ask how it is used and what it is used for. Ask what would happen if it wasn't used.

Explain that Satan has set temptations all around us. Although some temptations are passive, other temptations are actively seeking to penetrate and overcome us. These are like the mosquitoes that surround us when we are camping. Heavenly Father has given us gospel principles and commandments to help keep us safe. Remind the class that to be effective, gospel principles must be used.

Habits

Objective: To demonstrate how bad habits hinder our progress in this life.

Materials Needed: Four or five bricks.

Preparation: Wrap the bricks in plain paper and label them with a bad habit—gossiping, lying, smoking, etc.

Procedure: Ask a volunteer from the class to help you. Give him the bricks and explain that they represent the bad habits we laden ourselves down with. When we have so many bad habits, it becomes difficult to do those things which are good. Have the volunteer try to pick up the scriptures and read from them. It will be hard to hold anything else.

To make our journey back to Heavenly Father easier, we must lay aside our bad habits. It can be hard to forsake these bad habits, but in the long run it will make our journey much easier.

Habits

Objective: To illustrate that our daily actions lead to habits.

Materials Needed: Dominoes.

Procedure: During your lesson, line up a set of dominoes. Point out that when the first domino is knocked down, it in turn knocks down another, and so on.

Explain that habits work in the same fashion. One action leads to another. This develops into a pattern which once started is hard to break. Both good and bad habits work this way. Set the line of dominoes into action to illustrate your point.

Holy Ghost

Objective: To illustrate how we must learn to recognize the promptings of the Spirit.

Materials Needed: A poster board.

Preparation: Write a word or sentence in a foreign language on the poster board.

Procedure: Display the sentence and ask if anyone can read it. If no one is able to interpret the sentence, you translate the meaning. Point out that understanding a foreign language is not a simple matter. It requires time and effort to master it. Discuss what must be done (desire, good teacher, textbooks, use, commitment, etc.).

We will find that recognizing the promptings of the Spirit is much the same. We must first be willing to learn and obey in order to be able to understand. Discuss what we must do to reach that point (desire, commitment, scripture reading, prayer, fasting, church meeting and temple attendance, etc.).

Understanding the promptings and guidance of the Spirit in our life also requires a commitment of time and effort.

Holy Ghost

Objective: To show that following the Spirit will guide us through a perilous path.

Materials Needed: Many blocks or pieces of wood in different sizes.

Preparation: If desired, label each of the blocks with a different transgression or sin.

Procedure: Scatter the blocks on the floor in front of you. Ask one of the class members to walk through the blocks and stand by you. Offer encouragement from time to time. When the class member reaches the front, ask the class what could have happened if he had slipped on one of the blocks. (He could have fallen, he could try again, he could give up, etc.) Ask the class what helped him get through the blocks. (Sight.)

Discuss how worldly stumbling blocks can get in the way on our road back to Heavenly Father. Identify some of the stumbling blocks that fill our world (pride, worldliness, immorality, etc.) and who set them there (be sure to include the idea that even though Heavenly Father knows they are there he did not put them there). Explain that we can "pick" our way through the stumbling blocks by living righteously and "seeing by the Spirit." Discuss what must be done to achieve this.

Additional Idea: Talk about how keeping the commandments helps us receive the spiritual sight necessary to avoid the "stumbling blocks."

Humility

Objective: To show that humility can help us be more in tune with the Spirit.

Materials Needed: Two clear glasses, very hot water, ice water, and liquid food coloring.

Procedure: Place ice water in one glass and hot water in the other. Drop food coloring into each of the glasses. Discuss with the class the difference the temperature of the water makes in the dispersion of the food coloring.

Explain that we are like the water. When we are warm and humble the Spirit of the Lord can color our lives more fully.

Individual Worth

Objective: To show that differences do not make one person better or worse than another.

Materials Needed: An apple, an orange, and a banana.

Procedure: Ask which of the fruits you display is better than the others. Ask for personal favorites. Explain that even though you might like one kind of fruit better than another, it does not take away from the value of the other fruits; and explain that not everyone will prefer the same kind of fruit over another.

Liken the fruit to people. People are just a little different from each other in personality and in physical stature, but that does not lessen their worth to their Father in Heaven.

Individuality

Objective: To help us accept the differences in others.

Materials Needed: A jigsaw puzzle.

Procedure: Ask the class members if they have ever put together a jigsaw puzzle. Point out that it's interesting to note that the pieces are all different, yet they fit together to form beautiful pictures. Ask if any of the class members have put together a puzzle and found that one piece was missing. Suggest that this causes feelings of disappointment and frustration.

Explain that as children of our Heavenly Father, we are also all different. These differences offer the variety that makes the world an interesting and exciting place. By cooperating we can all work together and accomplish many wonderful things. All of us are an important part of this divine picture. Even the absence of one individual leaves this picture incomplete.

Variation: Pass out all the pieces of a large puzzle to illustrate how each member of the group must contribute to make the picture complete.

Inspiration

Objective: To demonstrate the effect of personal inspiration in our lives.

Materials Needed: An alarm clock.

Procedure: Display the alarm clock. Ask the class if they ever lie in bed and, without looking at the clock, know that the alarm is about ready to go off? Point out that those instinctive feelings can be very strong.

Draw a parallel between this and personal inspiration we receive. Explain that we can be prompted or inspired to say or do things without prior thought. The feelings can be just as strong as the intuitive knowledge that the alarm clock is due to go off.

Integrity

Objective: To show why regular maintenance of our integrity is important.

Materials Needed: Building blocks.

Preparation: Label each block with a positive characteristic of integrity.

Procedure: As you build a wall of building blocks, explain that personal integrity is made of small everyday actions that help build a barricade against Satan. As we actively increase and maintain our integrity the barricade becomes thicker and higher (continue to build the wall).

Then point out that Satan's ultimate plan is to completely destroy our barricade of integrity so that we will be in his power. To achieve this he first weakens the outside, "nonessential" part of our integrity (remove a few "outer" blocks). As we come to accept this erosion of our integrity, he begins to take bigger and more important chunks (follow with appropriate actions to the wall of blocks) from our integrity until the barricade we have carefully built crumbles.

Our goal, then, is to never give Satan a chance to weaken our wall of integrity. Discuss ways to build and maintain personal integrity.

Integrity

Objective: To show how reading the scriptures is important to integrity.

Materials Needed: Sugar cubes and royal icing.

Preparation: Build a wall using sugar cubes with royal icing as a mortar and another wall using sugar cubes only.

Procedure: Show the class the two walls and ask if anyone can see a difference in the walls. Demonstrate that the mortared wall cannot be easily tipped over and that the wall without the mortar is easily broken.

Explain that reading the scriptures is the glue or mortar in our wall of integrity. Our wall is then more durable and lasting. Discuss how reading the scriptures can support our growing integrity.

Integrity

Objective: To demonstrate that small acts of dishonesty erode our integrity.

Materials Needed: A tray of dampened dirt (a cookie sheet works well), a tin can, and water.

Preparation: Punch small holes in the bottom of the tin can.

Procedure: Suggest that many people believe that small acts of dishonesty do not affect our overall integrity. Explain that integrity is like the dirt in the pan and that dishonesty is like the water. At this point pour the water into the can and let the water sprinkle onto the dirt.

Explain that small acts of dishonesty build up and begin to erode integrity a little at a time until major parts of integrity are washed or eroded away. Discuss what might be meant by "small acts of dishonesty."

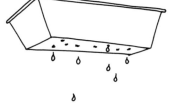
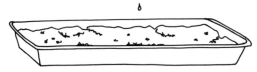

Judging

Objective: To show that judging another person's actions can lead to inaccurate conclusions.

Materials Needed: Several sizes of shoes.

Procedure: Have one class member take off his shoes. Have him put on a pair that might be too small and walk around the room. Now have him try on several other pairs of shoes, repeating the process each time. Ask him how his feet feel (tired, sore, uncomfortable) and if he would like his own shoes back.

Explain that we must be careful not to view anyone else's actions through our own experiences. Sometimes if we were to "walk in his shoes" we might find ourselves pinched and unable to cope with their problems, or even their successes.

Knowledge

Objective: To illustrate that knowledge must be obtained through proper channels.

Materials Needed: Several books relating to medicine.*

Procedure: Show the books to the class. Explain that you have decided to become a doctor and that these books will help you achieve that goal. Ask if holding the books will give you the ability to be a doctor. Will carrying them for a week or so give you the knowledge you need? The answers to these two questions will obviously be no. Discuss why not.

Explain that knowledge is not gained that way. In order to gain knowledge it is necessary to put forth effort and study from the *correct* books.

Additional Idea: Include one book with information from another field (mechanics, for instance). Explain that studying from this book will *not* give us the correct (medical) knowledge.

*Any profession (engineering, computer technology, etc.) will work well.

Love

Objective: To illustrate how love binds us together.

Materials Needed: Individual links for a paper chain.

Procedure: Pass to each class member an individual link for a paper chain. Point out that these links represent each person. Explain that if they were to try and make a chain they couldn't because there is nothing to bind the links together. Now pass around additional strips of paper and a stapler. These additional pieces of paper represent love. Use these strips of paper to loop through two links and bind them together. Allow the class to fashion a chain after this pattern. Explain that love is a powerful way that we can bind ourselves together as a group.

Magnifying Your Calling

Objective: To demonstrate that magnifying your calling is best accomplished one step at a time.

Materials Needed: A tape measure.

Procedure: Select a class member to assist you. Ask him to take a step and you will measure it. Tell the class how many inches he stepped. Now ask him to take a larger step. Measure the step and tell the class how far he went this time.

Ask your helper what he had to do to take a bigger step and whether it was difficult. You can include ideas such as moved foot further, used more energy, tried harder. Ask the class what would happen if he kept taking bigger steps. (He would go further.)

Liken this action to magnifying your calling. Explain that this is best accomplished by doing a little extra all the time as opposed to making one giant leap forward. Discuss what can be done to magnify different callings in life.

Missionary Work

Objective: To show that sharing the gospel brings more light to a darkened world.

Materials Needed: Several flashlights.

Procedure: Show the class that you have several flashlights in a bag (keep one out). Turn on your flashlight and turn off the classroom light. Ask the class what would happen if you turned off your light. Now give one of the extra flashlights (turn it on first) to another person in the room. Ask what this does to the room and why. Continue to hand out the flashlights until all are passed out. Discuss briefly how the many flashlights make the room brighter and a better place to be.

Explain that the flashlights are like the gospel of Jesus Christ. The gospel brings light into our lives and, when we share it, it can bring more light into a "darkened" world, making it a better place to live. Discuss ways that we can share the gospel.

Additional Idea: (This idea is excellent but not appropriate for every class and must be done with prayerful application.) Give flashlights to everyone except one or two. Ask those one or two if they would like a flashlight. Explain that you are sorry but you didn't have time to get them one. Ask them how they feel. Now, while you are handing them their flashlight, explain to the class how it would feel to go before the Savior and explain that you could not share the gospel because you didn't have time. This could lead to a lesson on perspective.

Missionary Work

Objective: To teach that everyone can receive the light and love of the gospel through our missionary efforts.

Materials Needed: A flashlight and a mirror.

Procedure: Briefly explain to the group that by using the mirror you can reflect the beam of light to various areas of the room. Give a quick demonstration or have a class member help. Select a target point in the room, then use the mirror to direct the beam to that place (practice before). Tell the group that even the darkest area of the room that has never received light can be reached. It may take time and thought and effort to get around obstacles and figure out which angle to use, but all areas can be reached.

Liken this to missionary work. With Christ as our light source, we act as the mirror which reflects the love and truth he offers. We can reflect this to all of our Heavenly Father's children. There are so many who have lived in darkness all their lives. To us they may appear unapproachable, impossible to reach. Yet we learn from this lesson that they too can receive the light. It may take a great deal of time and effort as we search for ways to reach them, but with diligence and faith we can be successful.

Ordinances

Objective: To illustrate what the saving ordinances are and how they are vital to our lives.

Materials Needed: A set of four keys.

Procedure: Take the first key and explain that it represents baptism. When we are baptized, we receive a key which can be used to unlock a door on our journey back to Heavenly Father.

The second key is the priesthood. Although it is held by men, it must be shared with women and family members to unlock the second door on the journey.

The third key is temple endowments. This key unlocks the next door, enabling us to draw ever closer to our Father in Heaven.

The last key is temple marriage. With the use of this key we unlock the final door on our journey to return home.

The keys represent the saving ordinances vital to exaltation. Receiving the keys represents the sacred acts of the ordinances. Actually using the keys to unlock the doors illustrates that we are living worthily. Obtaining and using these keys must be done in order.

Parenting

Objective: To encourage us to spend time teaching our children.

Materials Needed: A large screw and a large nail.

Procedure: Discuss the differences in using screws and nails when building. Ask which is quicker to use. (The nail.) Point out that with a couple of swift blows from a hammer, you can drive the nail into the wood. The screw requires more time to use. With slow, steady twists of the screwdriver you gradually work the screw down into the wood. Ask which holds the pieces of wood together longer and tighter. (The screw.) Explain that the screw is constructed so that the small ridges of metal dig into the wood and hold the wood firmly in place. In most cases it requires almost as much effort to remove it as to put it in. The nail on the other hand can very quickly be pried loose. More effort must be exerted in initially using the screw, but its benefits are much longer lasting.

Explain that teaching children offers a similar situation with time and effect. We can take a few quick opportunities to teach basic principles to our children, and at first the results seem pleasing. However, with a slight amount of pressure we will find that these principles could easily be loosened.

Tell the class that by using teaching moments we can gradually work these basic principles into our children's everyday lives. Then these principles will not be easily removed. If our teaching is a slow and steady journey throughout childhood, we will find the principles have been gradually ingrained into their lives. The time and effort it takes will prove worthwhile in the future.

Scripture Reference: Proverbs 22:6; Deuteronomy 6:7.

Patriarchal Blessing

Objective: To illustrate that our patriarchal blessings are loving instructions from our Father in Heaven.

Materials Needed: An addressed, stamped envelope.

Procedure: Have the group imagine themselves far away in a foreign land. They have been away for a long time and feel lonely and isolated. Have them imagine their joy at receiving a letter from home. They'd most likely read it again and again, savoring every word.

Explain that in a sense, we are as strangers in a foreign land. But we have the opportunity of receiving a very special letter from home; one which offers divine guidance, instruction, and encouragement. This letter is our patriarchal blessing, and it is sent from our Heavenly Father to a child whom he loves dearly.

Perspective

Objective: To show that we can lose the simple part of the gospel in everyday living.

Materials Needed: A statue or picture of Jesus Christ and several light scarves.

Procedure: Place the statue of Christ in the center of the table. Make sure that the table is not otherwise cluttered. Tell the class how important Christ is in your life and how much you want to always listen to what he says. Then tell them that you would like them to listen to one of your typical days.

Tell a story about a *very* busy and hectic day. Fill it with good activities (Relief Society meeting, priesthood activity, taking children to music lessons, fixing a bike for a child, making a birthday cake, attending an adult education class, exercising, etc.). Be sure not to find time for prayer, scripture study, or compassionate service. As you tell about each activity, drape a scarf over the statue of Christ. Do this until you have finished with the entire day.

Explain to the class that you had a day filled with good, "gospel-approved" activities, but the real center of the gospel was covered with the busy things of life. Prayer, scripture reading, meditation, compassionate service, all the things that help us listen to the promptings of the Spirit and become closer to Jesus Christ—the truly important things—were not there.

Discuss how perspective can help us uncover the basic gospel principles and keep our lives simple.

Perspective

Objective: To show that the most important things cannot be bought with money.

Materials Needed: A dollar bill.

Procedure: Hold the dollar bill in front of the class and ask what it can buy. Using one side of the chalkboard, list as many suggestions as possible. Remind the class that if saved and used with other dollar bills, it can buy many other things.

Now ask if all things can be bought with money. Discuss what things cannot be bought with money (friendship, love, priesthood, temple marriage, etc.). List these items on the other side of the chalkboard.

Ask the class which of these things would be the most lasting. Discuss why.

Additional Idea: Explain that even though some things cannot be obtained with money, there is a price (or sacrifice) that must be paid. Discuss what must be done to obtain each item (friendship, love, priesthood, temple marriage, etc.).

Potential

Objective: To illustrate the limitless potential we have as individuals.

Materials Needed: Yarn, knitting needles, and knitting instruction book.

Procedure: Display your materials and explain that with the proper materials, tools, and instructions you can make a wide range of things. The items that you could create with the yarn are almost limitless. Or the materials can sit in your closet and never reach their potential.

Our own lives hold an even greater potential. Heavenly Father has given us this life to use as we choose. He has also given us a means by which we can create something magnificent. Scriptures, prophets, Church auxiliaries, and patriarchal blessings are but a few of the tools he has given us to aid us in this great endeavor. We can make of our lives whatever we desire, or we can sit idly by. The choice is ours.

Preparation

Objective: To encourage us to be prepared in all things.

Materials Needed: A cup.

Procedure: Point out that the cup is perfectly good and useful. However, to someone who is thirsty the empty cup would be worthless.

Explain that we can be good and useful servants for our Father in Heaven. However, if we are not prepared spiritually, we can offer no comfort or guidance to those in need. If we are not prepared with our food storage, we can offer no food to ease the pains of those who are hungry. We must be prepared in all areas to prove ourselves faithful servants.

Preparation

Objective: To demonstrate the value of being prepared.

Materials Needed: A large rubber ball.

Procedure: Invite a class member to help with this demonstration. Have them stand a few feet in front of you. Tell them to keep their hands by their sides the entire time. Gently toss the ball to them. They won't be able to catch it because their hands are down. Ask the class why they didn't catch it. (Because their hands were down. They were not prepared.)

Next instruct them to stretch out their arms. Gently toss the ball again. They will be able to catch it this time. Point out that this is because they were prepared when the ball came to them.

Ask how many times we simply keep our hands at our sides rather than making the effort to prepare. Prior preparation is vital in all areas of our lives. Achieving success depends largely on our being prepared.

Program Changes

Objective: To show how program changes can be effective.

Materials Needed: One old-fashioned wood tool (manual) and one newer wood tool of the same variety (electric).

Procedure: Show the tools and ask what their use might be. Indicate that the older tool was very modern in its own time and then discuss the similarities and the differences between the tools. Explain that even though the tools are different, their basic use is the same. Tell the class that the most important thing is not the tool but how it is handled and what is the ultimate goal for its use. Point out that both tools can be used to turn out quality or junk, depending on the user or the goal.

Explain that these tools are like program changes that occur from time to time. Program changes must be used correctly, with the ultimate goal constantly in mind for the most effective use. Tell the class that even though the program has changed, the ultimate goal has not.

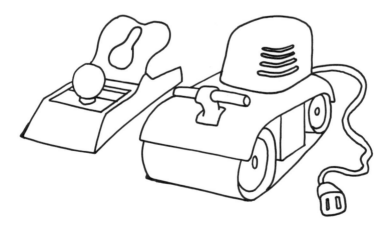

Purity

Objective: To show that purity is desirable.

Materials Needed: Dirt and rock salt.

Procedure: Place the rock salt on a plate and pass it around the class for sampling. Tell the class about the purity of salt and, if time permits, give some historic background on the importance of salt. Now take an equal amount of dirt and mix it into the rock salt. Pass the plate around again and offer samples. Ask why no one wants to sample the salt.

Explain that we are like the salt. When we are pure before the Lord we can be worthy servants, but if we allow ourselves to become soiled in any way we lose that ability. Talk about what could cause impurity and how it can be avoided.

Additional Idea: This lesson can lead to one on repentance by your talking about what steps need to be taken to make the salt pure again and comparing them to the steps of repentance.

Repentance

Objective: To show that repentance must be used correctly in order to gain eternal life.

Materials Needed: A small chest with a padlock and a key.

Preparation: Lock the padlock.

Procedure: Show the chest and state that inside is the eternal joy that we all seek. Explain that you will not be able to reach that eternal joy because a sin has locked the box.

Show the key. Explain that Heavenly Father has given us a way to rid ourselves of sin and unlock the box so we can achieve eternal joy. This key is called repentance.

State that we can see the key or hold it or even put the key into the lock, but until we *use* the key the box will remain locked and the treasure we seek will be unavailable. Demonstrate with the key and padlock as you speak.

You may want to expand on the principles and methods of repentance.

Additional Idea: Try to use the key upside down or backwards. Suggest the idea that the key must be used *correctly* in order to really work. Discuss what true repentance is (anguish, godlike sorrow, change of heart, etc.) and what it is not (just saying, "I'm sorry").

Repentance

Objective: To illustrate that repentance must be administered through the correct channels in order to be effective.

Materials Needed: A bottle of prescription medication and a bottle of nonprescription medication (both the same type if possible).

Procedure: Show the two bottles of medicine and ask how they are different. Explain that the prescription medication must be prescribed by a doctor and is usually stronger for a more serious illness. Discuss what would happen if we used only the nonprescription medicine. Be sure to include the idea that the medicine might not work as well or that we wouldn't get well as quickly or we may not get well at all.

Explain that repentance is like the medicine. Sometimes we must go to a priesthood authority (bishop or stake president) for counsel and guidance toward forgiveness. When this is the case, "nonprescription" repentance will not be effective. Discuss why and/or bear testimony of repentance through priesthood authority.

Repentance

Objective: To encourage us to use the process of repentance.

Materials Needed: An eraser.

Procedure: Ask the class to suppose that at the beginning of each school year each student was given an eraser to use. When a mistake was made, the eraser would be used to correct it instead of writing over it or crossing it out. This would allow the student to correct the error and learn from it. It would not be important how much of the eraser was left at the end of the year. What would matter would be that it was used each time it was needed. Therefore, even a student who made many errors could finish the year successfully.

Explain that as children of God we have been given an eraser to take care of our mistakes. It is repentance. It is important that we don't cover up or ignore our shortcomings. We must use the process of repentance to correct the errors in our lives. In the end it will not matter how often we have had to rely on repentance. What will matter is whether we did repent every time it was needed. By doing this we can finish this earth life successfully.

Repentance

Objective: To show the value of repentance.

Materials Needed: A glass.

Preparation: Make sure the glass is clean and clear. Lightly oil or cream your hands just before the lesson.

Procedure: Display the glass and ask if the class would feel comfortable serving someone a beverage in it. Tell your class it represents our lives. Pick up the glass and then set it back down. Your set of fingerprints will be noticeable. Explain that there are times when we handle our lives carelessly and give in to temptations. Point out that sin leaves its mark on our lives. However, sometimes we don't feel that one mistake makes a difference, and we fail to use repentance. Then it is easier to give in to temptation again. Pick up the glass in a different spot and set it back down, leaving another set of fingerprints. State that when we continue our lives without repenting, our mistakes take their toll. As you talk, repeat the process of picking up the glass. Change it from hand to hand two or three more times. When you finally put the glass down it will be covered with fingerprints. Now ask the group who would feel comfortable serving beverages in this glass. If we don't use repentance, our lives become so clouded with mistakes that we are no longer able to offer the Lord the service we should.

Variation: You may take this lesson one step further and use a spray cleaner to wipe away the fingerprints to illustrate the way repentance can wipe away mistakes.

Reverence

Objective: To help us understand that failing to be reverent can distract others from feeling the Spirit.

Materials Needed: A small piece of thread.

Procedure: Place a piece of thread on the front of your shirt or jacket prior to your lesson. It should be of a color which will stand out easily on your clothing. Begin your lesson on reverence. At an appropriate point, stop and ask if anyone noticed the thread. You will be surprised at the number of people who will respond. Find out if it bothered them. You'll find that a good portion of the class will have been so distracted by the thread that they paid little attention to your lesson.

If something as little as a thread could keep us from listening in a meeting, how much more distracting is talking, tapping a foot, or any other form of inappropriate behavior or appearance? Our lack of reverence can distract others from the spirit of the occasion.

Sacrifice

Objective: To point out that through sacrifice we gain an appreciation for our blessings.

Materials Needed: A glass of ice water.

Procedure: Display the glass of ice water and ask the class if the water appears desirable. Most will express a fairly positive attitude toward it. Then ask them to imagine that they have been working in the garden on a hot summer day. There is no shade. They are bent over pulling weeds all afternoon. They are sweating and their mouth is dry from the dust. Ask them how desirable the glass of water will appear after this hard day of work.

State that we experience a similar feeling in life when we sacrifice time, effort, or means for any good thing. This holy act of sacrifice leads us to a greater appreciation of what we do have. It helps us focus on our many blessings that we take for granted.

Scouting

Objective: To show that Scouting is best when equally supported by the boy, the parents, and the leaders.

Materials Needed: A three-legged stool and three word-strips—the boy, the parents, the adult leaders.

Procedure: Show the stool and ask what would happen if one of the legs was missing (the stool would fall). Ask what would happen if one of the legs was shorter than the other two (the stool would be wobbly).

Explain that the stool is like Scouting. To really be an effective and stable program the three groups must understand and be prepared to act in the program. Put up each wordstrip and explain what responsibilities each person has.

Sum up your lesson by returning to the stool and explaining again the importance of each group working in the program.

Scriptures

Objective: To help us realize the importance of reading our scriptures daily.

Materials Needed: A recipe card.

Procedure: Display the recipe card of a favorite dish and tell the class what a recipe is (a set of instructions to prepare food). Tell the class that at times you can be tempted to cook without referring to a recipe, especially if the recipe is used often.

However, if you haven't used a recipe for a long time you would be unable to remember the proper ingredients. Tell them that even a slight difference can cause the recipe to fail. To ensure the item turns out its very best and to save time and ingredients from being wasted on unsuccessful attempts, it is vital to refer carefully to the recipe each time.

Explain that Heavenly Father has given us the scriptures to use as instructions for successful living. It is important to refer to them often. To vary even slightly from his directions can result in serious consequences. To aid us in our eternal progression we must read our scriptures often, using them as a recipe for our lives.

Scripture Reference: Doctrine & Covenants 33:16; 2 Timothy 3:16.

Scriptures

Objective: To show that the scriptures can protect us if we use them.

Materials Needed: An umbrella and the scriptures.

Procedure: Hold up a closed umbrella and ask what it is used for. Be sure to include the idea of protection from the elements. Ask the class what must be done before the umbrella is a protection (open the umbrella and use it). Demonstrate and explain that, if used correctly, the umbrella can protect us even when the storm around us is strong.

Put the umbrella down and hold up the scriptures. Liken the umbrella to the scriptures. Remind the class that to be a protection, the scriptures must be opened and used. The scriptures were given to us to be a protection from all the storms of life, but they must be used properly to be most effective.

Additional Idea: This object lesson can be used for almost any gospel principle or even the gospel generally. Simply use your gospel objective in place of "scriptures."

Self-Esteem

Objective: To show that the little everyday things can eat away at our self-esteem if we are not careful.

Materials Needed: A silhouette of a face.

Procedure: Show the silhouette. Explain that during the day little things can tear away at our self-esteem. Discuss what some of these little things could be. As you enumerate some of these belittling things, tear little pieces of the silhouette away until you are left with a misshapen face. Explain that when we allow these outside "influences" to tear at our self-esteem we can become insecure, unhappy, or even emotionally handicapped. Discuss ways to prevent this from happening.

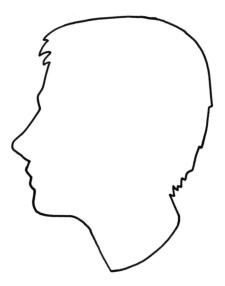

Service

Objective: To help us understand that through service we can reach our full potential.

Materials Needed: A wind chime.

Procedure: If possible, hang the wind chime up before the lesson. Point out to your class how pretty it is to look at. Ask: But when does it exhibit its true beauty? (When the wind blows.) As the breeze sets the wind chime moving, we can become enchanted with the lovely sounds it offers. The movement of the chime gives it a much greater value.

Suggest that in some ways we are the same as the wind chime. We can take care of our outward appearance. We may put our very best foot forward with our looks. But the true key to our worth is missing. Tell the class that through service others are allowed a glimpse of a deeper beauty in us. A love will radiate to others as we serve. Service enables us to reach our full potential as individuals.

Service

Objective: To illustrate that serving others increases our capacity to love, as well as our desire to continue to serve.

Materials Needed: An old pair of shoes and a new pair of shoes.

Procedure: Show the class members the new pair of shoes and discuss how it feels to wear new shoes. The leather and soles are stiff and it can be quite uncomfortable to wear them. But gradually with use they become "broken in" and it is much easier to wear them for longer periods of time. Display the old shoes. Explain that eventually, through regular use, the leather has softened, making it more flexible. The shoe now seems to have molded itself to the shape of the foot. We find ourselves passing by the newer shoes in our closet to wear our old favorites.

Liken this to service. As we begin to serve, it may be quite uncomfortable for us, but as we continue to serve we gradually become more relaxed and start to enjoy it. Eventually, just as with the old shoes, we develop a real love for service. We also gain a love for those we're serving and soon find that we welcome the opportunity to serve.

Service

Objective: To encourage us to have a positive attitude when serving.

Materials Needed: Refreshments.

Preparation: Prepare two sets of refreshments. The first set should appear unappetizing, as if not much thought or effort went into it. An example might be overdone sugar cookies. Prepare something for the second set which appears to have taken time and effort, is pleasing to the eye, and is tasty.

Procedure: Arrange to have someone come and serve the first set of refreshments. The individual serving should dress casually for the occasion (e.g., a sweatsuit). They should quickly and carelessly pass out the cookies. A few comments could be added to let the class know what an imposition it was to make and serve the refreshments. Do not offer napkins or other extras. The group should be rushed to finish.

Next serve the second set of refreshments. Take the time to make everything special (tablecloth, decorations, napkins, etc.). Make sure your appearance is neat and tidy. As you pass the refreshments make pleasant conversation with the members of your group. Sincerely compliment individuals and give each one special attention. Make them feel very important. Let them know how good it is to be with them. Express to them your gratitude for the opportunity to bring them a treat.

At the conclusion ask them how they felt after each set of refreshments. Then take a few moments to discuss with your class the importance of having a good attitude when offering service. Explain that those you're helping know whether you sincerely care by how you act and feel. Tell the class how good it made you feel to offer service when you took your time and made it special.

Sin

Objective: To show how sin can become a burden and how that burden can be lifted.

Materials Needed: Several filled bags that have straps or handles.

Procedure: Ask a class member to assist you. Explain that the bags or burdens are like sin. Begin to load the class volunteer with the burdens. Tell the class that the more "burdens" (sins) we carry, the harder it is to get around. Discuss how we can reach a point when there are so many sins that we don't know where to begin taking them off. Discuss how carrying a burden of sin can make you feel.

Tell the class that the person carrying the sin must *want* to give away their burdens before you can help him. Discuss how some sins must be confessed to proper authorities before the load can be completely lifted. If time permits, continue talking about the steps of repentance.

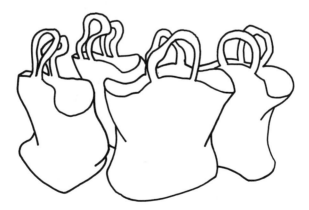

Spiritual Strength

Objective: To show that our personal testimony is important.

Materials Needed: Two people.

Procedure: Have two people stand in front of the class. Have one person lean against the other. Ask what happens when the support person moves. (The leaner falls down.)

Explain that our testimony is like the two people. At some point in our lives our testimony depends or leans on someone else's testimony (as children, new converts, etc.), but a time may come when the person we lean against might not be available. Ask everyone to think of someone who is spiritually strong—are they leaners? We can be a "leaner" or we can develop our own spiritual muscle and balance.

This object lesson will work either before or after a lesson on developing spiritual muscle (testimony).

Spiritual Strength

Objective: To show what must be done to achieve spiritual strength.

Materials Needed: Weight-lifting equipment.

Procedure: Show the weight-lifting equipment to the class. Ask what it is and what it is used for (building muscles). Discuss with the class how developing that muscle takes many dedicated hours of work. Ask what the benefits of this would be. Ask if there are any drawbacks.

Explain that this equipment can only strengthen a person physically. Ask what kind of "equipment" would help us build spiritual "muscle." Draw a parallel to the dedication it takes to achieve this goal. Ask what the benefits and drawbacks of spiritual "muscle" would be.

Standards

Objective: To help us see the reason for high standards.

Materials Needed: A piece of fencing wire.

Procedure: Ask the class to imagine that they have a prize horse and they live next to a busy road. Ask if they would let the horse roam free. Ask if they would build a haphazard fence. Would they secure it in a well-built fence? Suggest that naturally they would protect it by using a strong, tall fence. This isn't done to punish the animal but rather to keep it safe from all the dangers.

Explain that high standards act as the strong, tall, protective fence in our lives. This is one important reason for having high standards. We are valuable to our Heavenly Father. He desires to keep us safe and protect us from the ways of the world.

Stewardship

Objective: To show that stewardship demands wise and thoughtful decisions.

Materials Needed: A handful of wheat.

Procedure: Show the handful of wheat to the class. Tell them that it could be used for two things; 1) to grind up and use for food, or 2) to plant, grow, and harvest. Discuss these two ideas.

Explain that our lives are like the wheat. We are given stewardship over certain abilities, possessions, or talents in this life. Define stewardship (we have been given the choice of how to use them). Sometimes we must decide whether to use these stewardships immediately or to plant and nurture them until they bloom. Include ideas on planting and nurturing at the right time, etc., and choosing between two "rights."

Stewardship

Objective: To help us understand the meaning of steward-ship.

Materials Needed: Any object which you greatly value, such as a fine piece of crystal, a nice cassette recorder, etc.

Procedure: Show your class the item that means a lot to you. Tell them why it's important. Explain who gave it to you or how long it took to save your money for it. Suppose someone wanted to borrow it. You would only lend it to a person whom you trusted to be careful with such a special item. If they were to abuse it, you would feel deeply hurt and disappointed in their careless behavior as a steward of your goods.

Explain that when we came to earth, Heavenly Father trusted us to be wise stewards with this precious opportunity. We are his, and he cares deeply about us. To be careless with our time, activities, and general life-style hurts him. We need to be very mindful of our every action so that we might prove ourselves worthy caretakers of that which belongs to our Father in Heaven.

Stress

Objective: To teach us how to reduce stress.

Materials Needed: A glass, water, and ice cubes.

Procedure: Fill the glass of water to the brim. Point out that even though it is completely full you've not spilled any. If you are very careful, you can probably manage fine without having a mess. Then pop a couple of ice cubes into it. The water will overflow.

~~Explain that~~ we are like the glass of water. We oftentimes fill our lives to the brim with activities. As long as nothing unexpected happens we are fine. However, when anything unexpected comes into our already full lives (like the ice cubes), we can't cope with all of it. To reduce the stress and allow us to handle things in a positive manner it is important to leave enough free time and resources that we can be flexible.

Stress

Objective: To help us gain an understanding of stress and what causes it.

Materials Needed: A tasty, well-prepared meal or refreshment.

Procedure: Tell your group you have tried to prepare a delicious meal for them. Serve the meal and, as they are ready to eat it, tell them there is one thing you forgot to mention. They have only thirty seconds to eat it all. Take out your watch and say go. After the time is up, point out that what should have been a pleasurable experience was made stressful by trying to cram in too much in too little time.

Explain that this is often what we do in our own lives. We may have a very pleasurable experience before us; baptism, vacation, birthday, or free time. We then take that pleasant time and try to fit too much into it. This results in stress. It can literally ruin the experience.

Success

Objective: To illustrate that success is measured by what we overcome and accomplish in life.

Materials Needed: Any small household appliance or tool which has given you good service.

Procedure: Display your appliance and explain to the group what a good product it has been. Tell them how long you have owned it. Share any stories about times it was dropped or abused and still continued to work properly. Explain that the worth of this product has not been measured by the brand name it carries or the price it cost, but rather the continual service and the overcoming of mishaps.

Compare this to ourselves. Often we measure success by the position we hold or our wealth. Instead, true success can be assessed by what we have overcome in life and our ability to endure to the end.

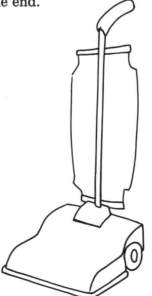

Talents

Objective: To illustrate the value of individual talents.

Materials Needed: Sample pieces of several types of fabric. Select a wide variety of fabric samples such as burlap, silk, denim, polyester, etc.

Procedure: Show the fabrics to the class and point out some of their differences. They look different as well as having varied uses. For instance, tell them burlap would be an excellent fabric for potato sacks. Silk is wonderful for formal wear, while denim makes great work pants. Each is different, each has a special use, and each is important to us. We need this variety to perform our various activities in life. A silk potato sack would not last very long. And a burlap evening gown would not be too comfortable.

Explain that as children of our Heavenly Father we are each different. Not only do we look different, but also we each have a different set of talents. All of these talents are important. Discuss what some of these differences could be (compassion, painting, listening, speaking, etc.). Point out that one person's talents do not necessarily qualify him for another person's responsibility. We need all of the talents that our Heavenly Father has given to his children. All are different but all have a special purpose, and all are important.

Teachability

Objective: To show how teachability is important in following the Savior.

Materials Needed: A lump of soft clay and a lump of hardened clay.

Procedure: Demonstrate how the soft clay can be molded into any shape that you desire. Then try to mold the hardened clay. Express the difficulty you are having in shaping the hardened clay. State that the hardened clay is unworkable.

Explain that we are like the clay. When we allow ourselves to be teachable we can be shaped and molded the way the Lord needs us. If we become stubborn we harden ourselves to the guiding influences of the Lord and we become unworkable. Discuss ways that we can become more teachable.

Teaching

Objective: To illustrate the importance of the Spirit in teaching.

Materials Needed: A hand puppet.

Procedure: Have the puppet displayed when class begins. Take a moment to talk about it, commenting on how cute it is, how much your children love it, and so forth. Also explain how many wonderful stories and lessons you've been able to give with the use of this puppet. However, no matter how cute or decorative this puppet is, no lesson can be taught with it simply setting idly on the shelf. Place the puppet on your hand to illustrate how it comes to life and can capture the audience's attention.

Explain that we will find similarities in our own teaching experiences. We may prepare our lessons in advance and know the material well. We can put hours into making our lessons decorative and attractive. Yet with all this effort on our part, we may still find the lesson turns out flat, not really touching the lives of our class members. The key to bringing our lessons to life and captivating the audience is the presence of the Spirit. We as teachers should diligently seek to teach by the Spirit. The Spirit enables us to teach lessons which can change the lives of our class members.

Teaching

Objective: To show how questions can aid a learning situation.

Materials Needed: Three slips of paper.

Preparation: Choose three similar objects (for instance, truck, tractor, car; or potato, carrot, celery). Write the names on the slips, one on each slip.

Procedure: Divide the class into three teams. Appoint a captain for each team and give each captain one of the previously prepared slips of paper. Tell everyone that each team must identify the object on the slip of paper.* You may want to tell them that each team has a different object.

Instruct Team One that the captain may give statements about his object (clues) but that *no* questions may be asked or answered. An example of a statement could be, "This object is large."

Tell Team Two that they may ask their captain questions but these can *only* be answered with a yes or no. An example of this type of question could be, "Is this object large?"

Team Three, however, may ask questions which require more complete answers. An example of this kind of question could be, "How large is this object?"

When the three objects have been identified, ask which team had access to the most information (it should be

Team Three). Discuss why. Explain that the way we use questions can be an aid in teaching. Discuss how questions and answers can lead to thought processes that can produce a strong foundation in knowledge.

*In the interest of time, you might set a time limit.

Teaching

Objective: To show teachers that doing is a better teaching tool than listening.

Materials Needed: A rope for each class member.*

Procedure: Give each class member a rope and have them put it under their chair. Demonstrate how to tie a particular knot with your rope. Have the class members take their ropes and, using the information you've already given them, tie a knot. Most class members will not be able to learn this skill quickly.

Now have the class members work with you, one step at a time, as you instruct them in another knot. Ask which way was easier.

*This will vary, depending on the skill you feel comfortable enough to teach: making paper airplanes, baking biscuits, making cookies, etc.

Teaching

Objective: To show that teaching is a means to helping others reach their full potential.

Materials Needed: A package of dehydrated food.

Procedure: Show the class the dehydrated food. Ask what this food needs. (Water.) When water is added the food swells up and reaches its full potential.

Explain that in a sense, as we teach others about the doctrines of Christ we offer them the water which will help them to swell and reach their full potential.

Scripture Reference: Doctrine and Covenants 10:66.

Temptation

Objective: To demonstrate the importance of avoiding situations which can cause us temptation.

Materials Needed: A magnet and a paper clip.

Procedure: Place the magnet a short distance from the paper clip. Slowly bring the magnet closer to it. Point out how the paper clip begins to wiggle and then is quickly drawn to the magnet. Try the demonstration again. As soon as you notice the paper clip begin to move, be prepared to quickly put your finger on it. This will keep the magnet from attracting it.

Liken this to ourselves when temptation is placed before us. If we linger in tempting situations, Satan will snare us quickly. To protect ourselves we must avoid these tempting situations or remove ourselves as soon as we perceive danger.

Testimony

Objective: To show the importance of having a testimony.

Materials Needed: A small piece of bark from a tree.

Procedure: Discuss briefly with your class the purpose of the bark on a tree. Point out that it protects the tree. If a tree loses too much bark, it can die from insects, exposure, and the loss of sap.

Explain that we have a similar protection in our spiritual lives. It is our testimony. A strong testimony can sustain us in times of turmoil. It can also keep us from giving in to temptations and doubts. Without a testimony we leave ourselves susceptible to the ways of the world.

Testimony

Objective: To illustrate the great influence our testimony can have in the lives of others.

Materials Needed: A container of a kitchen spice.

Procedure: Talk briefly to your class about spices. Explain that they are used to enhance the flavor of foods. Items which may not otherwise have been palatable become delicious when the proper spices are added. Those who are choosy eaters or who have no appetite can be enticed to eat foods which are good for them through the use of spices.

Tell the class that spices can quickly lose much of their flavor if they are not protected. To ensure their effectiveness we must take measures to keep them in airtight containers and use them regularly to rotate and replenish our supply.

Explain that our testimonies, just like spices, have a great influential power. Through their proper use, we can increase the desire of others to draw near to the Savior. However, we must exercise caution and protect our testimony. It is vital that we nurture it through study and faithfulness, or it will become a fragile thing, easily destroyed. If not used often, our testimony will not be as powerful and will lose the ability to affect the lives of others.

Testimony

Objective: To help us understand the importance of strengthening our testimony.

Materials Needed: A boiled egg, a dish of food coloring, and water.

Procedure: When class begins, explain that we are like the egg. The shell is like our testimony. We must carefully nurture our testimonies. If we don't try to strengthen our testimony, it will gradually weaken. And even a small weakness in it can be dangerous when we live in a world full of temptations and deceptions. Crack the shell of the egg and peel a small piece of it away.

Next place the egg in the food coloring solution and tell your class it represents temptations. While the egg is soaking, discuss for a few minutes the ways we can strengthen our testimony (e.g., sharing it, prayer, fasting, study, obedience).

Remove the egg and peel the shell away. The food coloring will have seeped in and stained part of the egg. Just as the cracked shell allowed this to happen, a weak testimony can let temptations slip into our lives.

Testimony

Objective: To show that a testimony must be cared for and strengthened all the time.

Materials Needed: A flashlight, a lamp, and a candle.

Procedure: Display the items on a table. Ask the class what they have in common. (They provide light.) Ask when they would probably be used. (At night.) Discuss why. Ask the class what they would do if the light suddenly went out at night. Ask how easy it would be to find a source of light in the dark. Discuss how knowing where the source of light is and what condition it is in helps us to be prepared.

Explain that our testimony is like the light. We seldom appreciate or even look for it in the daytime (good times). We really depend on our testimony during the difficult times in our life. Discuss why it is important to keep our testimony strong during the good times so that we will be prepared for difficult times.

Testimony

Objective: To illustrate the importance of sharing our testimonies with others.

Materials Needed: A bag and a potted flowering plant.

Preparation: Prior to class place the plant into the bag.

Procedure: When class begins explain to your group that there is a beautiful plant inside the bag. To share the full measure of the plant's beauty and fragrance it is necessary to take it out of the bag and display it. In addition the plant would eventually die in the bag, because it needs exposure to the sun.

Draw a similarity between the plant and our testimonies. It is not enough to simply have a testimony inside. For others to truly benefit from our testimonies, we need to share those testimonies with them. Our testimonies need constant exposure, or they too can wither and die.

Additional Idea: Substitute the idea of missionary work or example for testimony.

Thoughts

Objective: To show that our thoughts are important to our character.

Materials Needed: Two balloons, one helium filled and the other air filled.

Procedure: Be sure to have your balloons as much alike as possible. Hold one balloon in each hand. Discuss how the balloons are alike (size, color, shape, design, etc.). Tell the class that although they seem alike they are different in one important way—one is filled with helium. Ask how filling one with helium will make a difference.

Explain that we are like the balloons because what we fill ourselves with will determine whether we sink (drop the air-filled balloon) or soar (release the helium balloon). Discuss what thoughts can help us rise.

Time

Objective: To illustrate that organizing our time enables us to accomplish more.

Materials Needed: Several oranges, a large glass container, and water.

Procedure: Display the large glass container. Explain that it represents our lives, and that the oranges represent all the worldly activities that fill our lives and keep us busy. Invite the class members to list the different worldly things we have to do. Place an orange in the glass container for each activity they name. Squeeze as many oranges into the container as possible.

Point out that we often fill our lives with so many worldly activities that we don't seem to have any time for the spiritual things. Activities such as praying, reading the scriptures, attending Church meetings, and going to the temple may be absent from our lives.

Suggest that we might be surprised to find out there's a lot of time in our lives that is simply wasted. Take a pitcher of water and slowly pour the water over the oranges. The water will fill in all the gaps surrounding the fruit. You will be amazed at the amount of water that will fit into the container that was previously believed to be full.

Encourage the class members to seek out the wasted time in their lives and use it to increase their spirituality.

Truth

Objective: To enable us to realize how vital the truth is to our lives.

Materials Needed: Two identical containers, bleach, water, and a plant.

Preparation: Put water in one container and bleach in the other.

Procedure: As class begins, display the plant and place a container on each side of it. Tell the class that one container holds life-giving water for the plant and one holds poison that would kill it. Invite a class member to decide which container to use. Upon investigating, the person will be able to easily detect the bleach by its strong smell.

Explain that in our lives we have a similar choice between two things, truth or lies. We must have the truth to guide our lives by. If we are deceived, we can make decisions which can jeopardize our eternal future. Satan and his deceptions are very clever. We must be sure of our sources before randomly accepting something as truth. This choice is as vital to our lives as it was to the life of the plant.

Scripture Reference: John 14:6; Doctrine and Covenants 93:39.

Values

Objective: To show that eternal values help shield us from the forces of the world.

Materials Needed: Two rocks, water-base poster paint, an oil-base paint, two jars of water.

Preparation: Paint one rock with the water-base paint and the other with the oil-base paint. Try to paint both rocks in similar colors and patterns. Allow them to dry completely.

Procedure: Show the rocks to the class. Explain that even though they look similar there is an important difference: one rock's coloring is permanent.

Tell the class that you will now place a rock in each jar of water to help determine which is permanent.

While the rocks are soaking, ask the class if they know what a value is. Discuss values and explain the difference between worldly values (wealth, fads, and so on) and eternal values (chastity, love, and so on).

Take out the two rocks. Show the class that the water-base, or temporary, paint easily rubs off but the oil-base paint continues to "protect" the rock.

Liken the paint to values and the water to influences of the world. Discuss how eternal values can protect us from the negative influences of the world and help us reach eternal goals.

Additional Ideas: For other lessons, the idea of values can be replaced with the ideas of knowledge, scriptures, or spirituality.

Visiting Teaching/Home Teaching

Objective: To show the importance of visiting teaching or home teaching.

Materials Needed: One large box filled with several heavy objects.

Procedure: Have a class member try to lift the box. (Be sure he does not hurt himself.) Ask how it feels. Instruct two other class members to help the first lift the box. This will be easier.

Explain that the box is like the burdens we might carry in day-to-day life. Discuss what some of these burdens could be. When we become home teachers or visiting teachers we can help others with their day-to-day burdens.

Visiting Teaching/Home Teaching

Objective: To demonstrate the vital role of home teachers and visiting teachers.

Materials Needed: A wilted house plant and a fresh house plant.

Procedure: Display the wilted plant and explain that it is perishing because its caretaker has failed to provide life-giving water. Contrast it by showing the fresh plant. It has been well cared for and is therefore flourishing. Point out that we are caretakers of those we teach. If we fail to visit them regularly, we are neglecting their needs. By leaving them uncared for we allow them to become much more vulnerable to the enticings of Satan. However, if we follow up on their needs and progress, they can more easily grow and blossom under our attention.

Visiting Teaching/Home Teaching

Objective: To illustrate that what we put into visiting teaching or home teaching is what we will receive.

Materials Needed: Three clear glasses, clear fruit juice, and vinegar.

Procedure: Display the three glasses on a table. Tell the class that these goblets are very beautiful and of fine quality. Now pour vinegar into one and fruit juice into a second, leaving the third glass empty. Offer the glasses to a class member and ask him from which one he would rather drink. Tell the class that what you put into the goblets made the difference in its desirability.

Explain that visiting teaching and home teaching are like the glasses. No matter how beautiful the program is, it is what we put into it that makes it truly useful and desirable. If we put nothing into it we receive nothing in return. If we have a sour or negative attitude, we will receive a poor experience. If, however, we put our best effort into it, we can receive a wonderful feeling of fulfillment.

Additional Idea: As you discuss what goes "into" visiting teaching or home teaching you might want to use examples or illustrations.

Wisdom

Objective: To show that experience must be added to knowledge to make wisdom.

Materials Needed: A bowl filled with wheat or other whole grain.

Procedure: Ask what would happen if this grain was left in a dry place. Ask what would happen if it was planted and given water. Discuss.

Give a definition of wisdom (ability to judge what is right or true). Explain that the grain is like knowledge. To become wisdom, experience and time must be added. Ask how experience can make knowledge into wisdom.

Work

Objective: To encourage us to seek Heavenly Father's help in all we do.

Materials Needed: A hand eggbeater and an electric mixer.

Procedure: Ask the class if they were to mix up a cake batter, which tool they would rather use. Suggest that they could get the job done with the hand mixer, but it would take a lot more time to get the batter smooth. It would also prove to be very tiring. The electric mixer would be much easier to use. This is because they would be using an additional power source to help with the work.

Point out that oftentimes we try to do things on our own without enlisting the help from our Heavenly Father. He is there for us anytime we are willing to plug into the power source. We will find the burden to be lighter when we seek the guidance and strength of the Lord.

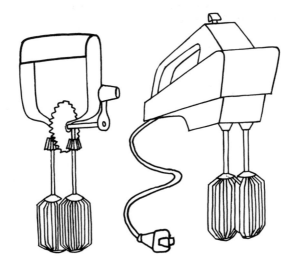

Young Women Program

Objective: To demonstrate the important roles in a successful Young Women's program.

Materials Needed: A triangle made of construction paper or cardboard.

Procedure: Put the triangle up in front of your group. Explain that the triangle is one of the strongest shapes known to man. It is often used in architecture. Buildings, bridges, etc., use the design of the triangle to reinforce and strengthen the structures. The triangle is strong because one side offers strength to the other and at the same time relieves the stress on the other two sides.

Tell the class that the Young Women's program is also like a triangle. There are three important roles; the leaders, the parents, and the young women. Each role supports the other and helps to relieve stress. Each role is vital. Designed in the shape of a triangle, if one side were missing the figure would collapse.

Subject Cross-Reference Guide